WILDERNESS FRUITS

WILDERNESS FRUITS

Eclectic Poems And Musings (Volume 2)

ZIRI DAFRANCHI

Heredita Press Limited

A CIP catalogue record is available from the British Library.
Ebook ISBN: 978-1-7398021-5-8
Paperback ISBN: 978-1-7398021-6-5

Hereditas Press
www.hereditaspress.com

WILDERNESS AND FRUITS

The wilderness is by nature a barren and an inhospitable place;
In life we sometimes go through a wilderness season:
And, surprisingly, we discover fruitfulness in an otherwise barren season.

Contents

Preface

The wilderness is a naturally barren and inhospitable place, it is a place that is uncultivated and unnatural for human habitation. A wilderness conjures up imagery of a vast expanse of land that goes on and on, seemingly without end. A jungle wilderness in contrast is a place filled with wild plants, thorny bushes, hidden and unusual creatures, with eyes blinking in the darkness, creating an eerie silence, where it is survival of the fittest and only the strong make it out alive. A wilderness is a place where most humans would not choose to tread, yet for some adventurous types a wilderness is a place of escape. Nonetheless, whether people seek it out as a once in a lifetime sojourn or somehow find themselves abandoned and wandering through it, a wilderness is the last place one would want to set up home, be it temporary lodgings or a long and drawn out stay. In a political context, a wilderness is a position of disfavour, a no-man's-land where it's difficult to attract public support. So too is the spiritual wilderness, which is regarded as a season of stagnation, insurmountable difficulties, challenges and even solitude. Whether it is due to misadventure, misfortune or being thrown in at the deep end, a wilderness for many is a real experience that some have unwillingly ended up far longer than intended or expected. Interestingly, some people who have wandered into the wilderness have been surprised to discover some form of life and productivity. Some people have found streams and fountains in the wilderness while others have discovered different fruit-bearing trees with an abundance

of fruits in season and even out of season. Thus bringing to life such
sayings as "beauty from ashes" and "treasures in the ruins."

"Wilderness experience" is a term used to describe a period when
people go through unusual and difficult challenges in life. It is a period
when people are stripped of the common pleasant things of life or are
simply unable to enjoy what they have whilst it is in their possession.
Very much like the natural wilderness, the wilderness experience is
usually characterised by little or no productivity, stagnation, and lack
of progress. And like the natural wilderness also, the wilderness
experience oftentimes yields fruits.

The *Wilderness Fruits* series is so titled because its contents
represent "fruits" that came out of my wilderness experience.
During the autumn of 2012, while recuperating from surgery due to a
health problem, my employment contract was suddenly terminated
and the company that I had worked for suddenly went into
liquidation. I couldn't have imagined it at the time, but this was the
beginning of my wilderness experience which would go on to last for
several years. This experience enabled me to spend some time
reflecting on life in all aspects and particularly my own life. These
reflections, as I spent much time studying, meditating, and praying,
culminated in a supernatural transformation which radically changed
my perspective on life and which I have been compelled since then to
share with others. During this period, I encountered a relationship
with God in a way that I could not have previously imagined which
brought about further spiritual enlightenment. Consequently, I began
to have a better understanding of my real identity including innate
abilities and talents I didn't know I had, as I also began to discover
parts of my purpose, including writing. And so I began to write.

As I wrote, the philosopher in me came to life and soon after the
poet in me also came alive. The product of my musings some of which
are presented as fictional stories are part of my wilderness fruits, as
well as my poems most of which were inspired by personal
experiences.

In *Wilderness Fruits* (Volume 2) you are served with a unique collection of my personal musings which are deeply insightful and inspirational (themes include wisdom, brokenness, hope, procrastination, time, focus, and right perspective), and also my retelling of some legendary wisdom fables (including Aesop's The Mountain in labour and The North Wind and The Sun) to reveal lessons which are relevant and applicable today. The poetry section comprises some of my soul-warming and thought-provoking collection of eclectic poems including some addressing social issues. A worthy collection of delicious exotic fruits to warm, soothe, and make merry your heart, and to tantalise, inspire and exercise your mind leaving you wanting for more.

I would like to take this opportunity to express my gratitude to God for turning my wilderness experience into a fruitful venture, and also to everyone who had supported me in one way or another during my wandering through the wilderness. I would also like to acknowledge and thank Joanna Basinga for an excellent edit, and also the wonderful staff of Hereditas Press for their professionalism throughout the production process.

Enjoy these wilderness fruits and be inspired.

Eclectic Poems

ECLECTIC POEMS

Global Village Life

GLOBAL VILLAGE LIFE

I

The Village's Goat

There was a goat collectively-owned by the village
Everybody knew that somebody should feed the goat
Which anybody out of everybody could feed
But nobody out of everybody was chosen
To feed the goat which anybody could

There was a goat collectively-owned by the village
Everybody assumed that somebody was feeding the goat
Which anybody out of everybody could feed
But nobody out of everybody chose
To feed the goat which anybody could

There was a goat collectively-owned by the village
Nobody ensured that somebody actually fed the goat
Which eventually died of neglect and starvation
Because nobody out of anybody did
What somebody who could be anybody should.

2

Golden Rule

Love yourself and love others as you love yourself
Be kind to yourself and be kind to others
Treat yourself right and treat others right
But don't treat others exactly as you'd like to be treated
Because we're all unique and differently made
And what might please us may displease another

One man's meat could be another man's pet
How right would it be to feed a man his pet
Just because it is meat to us?
How kind would it be to destroy someone's flowers
Just because to us they are weeds?
Why measure everyone with the same yardstick?

Life is simple but the world is complex
Not by its own nature but by our own design
The simple things we have made complicated
So we try to simplify the complex things
Like treating others as we like to be treated
And not as they would like to be treated.

3

Not A Rule

What you won't want others to do to you don't do to others
What you won't want others to say to you don't say to others
What you won't want others to say about you don't say about
others
What you won't accept from others don't give to others
So don't sow what you won't reap

If it will hurt you, it will hurt others
If it will demean you, it will demean others
If it will harm you, it will harm others
If it will enrage you, it will enrage others
If it will humiliate you, it will humiliate others
If it will make you feel unwanted, it will make others feel unwanted
If it will make you feel inferior, it will make others feel inferior
If it will leave you broken, it will leave others broken

This is not a rule

This is not just about race and racism
This is not just about sex and sexism

This is not just about age and ageism
This is not just about tribe and tribalism
This is not just about class and classism
This is not just about pride and prejudice
This is not just about ego and egoism
This is not just about isms and schisms

This is not a rule

This is about you and I
This is about being human
This is about being humane
This is about self-respect
This is about dignity
This is about the past
This is about the present
Most of all, this is about the future

This is not a rule

Time comes time goes; seasons come seasons go
Kingdoms come kingdoms go; empires come empires go
Powers come powers go; riches come riches go
People come people go, but the world remains
Same then and same now

This is not a rule; it is not a law
This is not a theory; it is not a formula
This is not an advice; it is not a strategy
This is the truth; this is wisdom
This is sense: common yet uncommon
This is life; this is hope
This is why we are the way we are
And this is why we must change.

4

Where Is The Love?

Me, me, me
My life, my way
I look after me. I just do me
It's all about me
So says every living "me"

But the world is not a world of mes alone
We have me, you, him, her and them
In a world full of multitudes of people
Who although individually are mes
Need you, him, her, and them to coexist

Hence we are all in this together
Which makes it about you and me
About him and her
And about them and everyone else
With whom we share the world

When I make it all about me
My response to his provocation
My disregard of her presence
My disdain of their juvenile behaviour
How might it affect those affected?

A rant might actually be a cry for help
And an aggressive tone a response to oppression
A stubborn disobedience might just be part of growing up
And a sexual deviant might be an abuse victim
We could help if we didn't make it all about us

We could prevent a suicide or murder
If we showed a little kindness
But if only for ourselves alone we cared
And another soul is lost as a result
Where is the love?

5

Nowadays

Back in the days it was a different tale
When one's back itched they turned to another
Who helped scratch their backs for relief
And if it was an animal's back that itched
It looked for a tree to rub against
To help scratch the itching

But nowadays it is a different tale
When an animal's back itches it looks for a human
Who would scratch its back to relieve the itch
And if a human's back itch he looks for a stick
Or any object which he uses to scratch it
To relieve the itching

Different tales for different times?
Have we evolved towards apathy for other humans?
And empathy for anything but humans?
Because while animals are housed and pampered in luxury
Humans are left roaming the streets homeless and hungry
And while we protest unfair treatments of animals
We care less about the brutalisation of fellow humans.

6

Prisoner Of Self

A person who takes away another's freedom
Is a prisoner to a far greater bondage
Because we could never truly be free
While holding another in bondage
To hold someone down we also have to stay down

The person who locks another in a room
Must ensure to remain in the house as guard
Otherwise the hostage could escape
Staying-put in the house as guard
Makes both hostage and guard prisoners

In disrespecting others, we disrespect ourselves
In treating others unequally, we treat ourselves unequally
In being unfair to others, we are being unfair to ourselves
In hating others, we become prisoners of hate
In setting others free, we set ourselves free

Because what we throw up must come down
What we push round will certainly come around
Every action attracts an equal and opposite reaction
Whoever digs a pit shall ultimately fall into it
And whoever throws a stone shall be hit by it.

7

Prisoner Of Conscience

Until we free our minds of hatred
Until we free our minds of malice
Until we free our minds of bitterness
Until we free our minds of envy
Until we free our minds of jealousy
Until we free our minds of wickedness
We will forever remain in prison

Until we free our minds of evil
Until we free our minds of greed
Until we free our minds of avarice
Until we free our minds of strive
Until we free our minds of rivalry
Until we free our minds of selfishness
We will forever remain in prison

Until we free our minds of racism
Until we free our minds of sexism
Until we free our minds of tribalism
Until we free our minds of nepotism
Until we free our minds of ageism
Until we free our minds of isms and schisms
We will forever remain in prison

Prisoner of conscience imprisoned by self
Chained by self-centred behaviours and attitudes
From which none but ourselves can free our own minds
It is time we freed our minds of ignorance
It is time we filled our minds with wisdom
It is time we freed our minds of every ism and schism
So that we will not forever remain in prison.

8

Legal Injustice

So the rogue Horse got caught
And got ridden by the Miss
While the Donkey who wronged not
Got burdened with the Master's load
And then there was the very naughty Zebra
Who in return only got a few stripes

A person commits an offence
But gets away lightly
Because of who or what he is
And another commits the same offence
But is heavily penalised
Again, because of who or what he is

A person kills, unseen and without a trace
And gets away with murder
Because there was not enough evidence
Another assaults someone in a public fight
And faces the full brunt of the law
Simply because there was compelling evidence

A person kills because he is licensed to kill
In return is awarded a medal of bravery
And publicly proclaimed a national hero
Another cleverly loots the national treasury
Because he was elected to serve
And is respected as a wealthy statesman

But another kills in self-defence
And is branded a villain and locked up for life
Another steals food to avoid starving to death
And is branded a rogue and vilified for life
And we call this legal justice
When in truth it is legal injustice.

9

Fighting For Freedom

I am a freedom-fighter fighting for freedom
Fighting on arrival, fighting for survival
Fighting because freedom is not free
Nor is it freely given by the oppressor
But must be demanded by the oppressed
From those who took away their freedom

I am a freedom-fighter fighting for freedom
Fight I must and fight I will
As I demand for freedom
I shall fight and not give up
Even when my demand is ignored
Till by any means necessary there is freedom

I am a freedom-fighter fighting for freedom
Better my fight than to live in bondage
So fight I will even if I must die
Because in fighting for freedom I am free
I am fighting against oppression
So that the oppressed will be free.

10

Bound In Freedom

Freedom is priceless but it isn't absolute
Unconstrained, freedom becomes a bondage
To be free to do all we please isn't freedom but bondage
Bondage itself is very costly and detrimental
But is also productive depending on perspective

There is bondage in freedom; self-restraint
There is also freedom in bondage; of the mind
Freedom and bondage are not mutually exclusive
Freedom exists in bondage and bondage in freedom
But we first need to know so to experience it

We can be free under bondage or freedom
When it is our choice to be free in the mind
And are truly free only when our freedom
Is bound in the freedom of self-restraint
Because to be bound in freedom is to be truly free.

11

To Be Free

The fowler's snare is broken but we are not escaped
The prison doors are open but we are not free
Why are we not free?
How can we be free when we're still in chains?

Oh, that the chains might be broken!
And we rouse ourselves shaking off the chains
Arising and walking through the open doors
To the freedom which awaits us if we rouse ourselves

Although the fowler's snare is broken
Although the prison doors are wide open
We could not be free still
Till we do what we need to do to be free

We need to awaken to the reality of our bondage
We need to arise from the slumber of ignorance
Drop the broken shackles and walk through the open door
Then we shall be free.

Not A Day For Poetry

Today is definitely not a day for poetry
As the sun cannot shine at night
Nor can the moon glow by day
Even if they would try to

Death is never announced with a joyful cry
Nor is birth reported with a mournful wail
The wicked have imagined vain things
And the heathens loudly roar in rage

Now the mighty have fallen mightily
As princes roam the streets barefooted
And the nobles are reduced to begging
While beggars ride on expensive horses

Oh, the charming beauty of this ugliness
The debilitating weakness of this strength
The sheer foolishness of this wisdom
So wantonly displayed with great pomp

Such that even the blind can see it as clearly
As the deaf can hear it loudly
Write I should but write I will not
Because today is not a day for poetry.

13

Africa, Our Africa

The poor people suffer miserably
As the monkeys work very hard
While the baboons enjoy the harvest
And everyone pretends to be happy

A people are invaded and conquered
Their heritage destroyed and pillaged
While they are reduced to servitude
And all pretend to be friends

A people are abducted and enslaved
Cargoed and shipped abroad as slaves
Exploited and dehumanised for centuries
And everyone pretends it's just a story

Freed, their descendants are oppressed
Labelled and treated as inferior
While their cry for justice is ignored
And everyone pretends all is well

Africa wails and groans in agony
Under the burden of exploitation
As the world preys and feeds on her
And everyone pretends she's fine

When Africa eventually collapses
After she's been milked dry and out
It is the world that will take the fall
Because Africa is collectively our Africa.

14

Simply Human

We are humans and not black or white
We are humans and not yellow or brown
We are humans and not Asian or American
We are humans and not European or African
We are truly simply human

We are humans and not items or products
Which can be branded or labelled
We are humans and not merely statistics
Used to make up the world's demography
We are truly simply human

We are humans and not tools or instruments
Which can be used for political motives
We are humans and not biological weapons
Used to wage religious and political wars
We are truly simply human

We are humans and should refuse to be manipulated
We are humans and should refuse to be objectified
We are humans and should refuse to be used or abused
We are humans and should refuse to be branded
We are truly simply human

15

Brainwashed

At first you were simply a human
First of a kind, basic, primitive but original
Then you learnt, you grew, you developed
You invented, improved, and advanced
An originator in the Land of Origins

Then they heard
And they came, they saw, they marvelled
Then they learnt, borrowed, and copied
But they didn't conquer
And so they returned

Then they said you're black (You believed)
They said they're white (You believed)
They said you're primitive (You believed)
They said they're civilised (You believed)
They said you need help (You believed)
They said they'll help (and You believed)

So they started to "educate" you
That the Saviour is white (You believed)
And the Devil black (You believed)
Angels are white and Demons black (You believed)
So they are good (You believed)
And you are bad (You believed)

Then they sold you their ways
Their version of what they took from you
Teaching you to speak like them
To eat and drink like them
To dress and look like them
So you can be a version of them

Now you're like them
(but not one of them)
You even think like them
(but for them not for you)
And you love everything of them
(but despise anything of you)

An identity lost, a history forgotten
How the mighty have fallen!
The prince has become the pauper
And the beggar the master
But only because you believed.

16

Black And White

Black and white the imaginary shades
Separating sisters from sisters
And turning brothers against brothers
Till humanity at last they've divided

Black and white the fictitious tones
Our skin colours are defined by
Although we're all shades of brown
And none is truly white or black

White and black the deceptive weapon
Devised and used to manipulate
Into hating and killing one another
But only because we are ignorant.

17

White Against Black

We are white and superior
They are black and inferior
We are white and good
They are black and evil
So we must keep them subjugated

Our duty is to control them
They cannot triumph over us
Good never succumbs to evil
But evil is overcome by good
So we must keep them dominated

Our right is to rule over them
Because we are superior
We must deny them power
Because they are inferior
So we must keep them subjected

You are white and superior
They are black and inferior
You are white and good
They are black and evil
So we should simply believe you?

18

White Privilege

To live in the best neighbourhoods
But having to pay less
To be accepted by elite institutions
Even with lower grades
To be offered the best jobs
With little or no experience
Only because you are white
Is white privilege

To drive around in expensive cars
And not be stopped by the police
To commit heinous crimes
And be given a lighter sentence
To be easily reabsorbed into the society
After serving time in prison
Only because you are white
Is white privilege

To be able to live your life
Without being prejudiced
To be able to be yourself
And not be stereotyped
To be able to express yourself
And not be accused of incitement
Only because you are white
Is white privilege

To believe that you are superior
And others inferior
To be advantaged over others
But fail to acknowledge it
To benefit from white privilege
And yet deny its existence
Even if you refuse to accept it
Is white privilege.

19

Unbroken

Man to man is so unjust, we've seen
Men chained by men in hate
Women killed by women in anger
Humans dehumanised by humans for gain
On this planet we call our home

And still the downtrodden rise
Revealing that to chain is not to confine
As to oppress is not to conquer
And to be unbound is not to be free
The reason we remain unbroken.

20

Democracy

Government is a group of people
Authorised by the people over the people
To govern the people and country
For the benefit of the people

Democracy is government of the people
Chosen by the people to serve the people
For the interest of the people and country
This is what we ordered

Democrazy is government of the few
Selected by the few to dominate the people
Enriching the few at the expense of the people
This is what we got.

21

Politicking

Politicking is a game of tricking
Where votes are obtained by tricking
By people who are skilled in tricking
From people who are unaware of the trickery

Politicking is a game of tricking
Where voters, victims of the trickery
Are told what they want to hear, in trickery
By politicians who are masters of trickery

Politicking is a game of tricking
Where politicians having won by trickery
Break the promises they made in trickery
To people who remain unaware of the trickery.

22

War For Peace

The world is at war
Because it is not at peace
And for world peace
We go to war

The war for peace
The world must fight
With no stone unturned
Till peace is found

The cost of peace
Is paid with wars
Which is why
The world is at war.

The Life We Live

THE LIFE WE LIVE

23

Tagged

We come into the world without a name
But with an identity unknown to all
Unknown to all including ourselves
Until we eventually uncover who we are
Which might not be truly reflected by
The name we are given after we are born

The name Wisdom don't make wise the bearer
Nor can Richie make rich the bearer
Because a name is a tag for identification
But is not a definition of our identity
Which is more than any name we bear
The name we are given after we are born

We come into the world without a title
With or without which we still are
Who we are created to be
And can do the things we are born to do

We can lead without the tag of leader
And heal without being tagged a doctor

A name is more or less a tag
As are the titles we acquire
Which may fall short of our true identity
Or the purpose for which we exist
The hood does not make a monk
Who without a hood is still a monk

The person who teaches is a teacher
With or without the title of teacher
While a person who fails to teach
Is not a teacher even if titled a teacher
Names and titles don't mean much
If we failed to live up to them

Low esteem desires the purple robe
As an end not a means to an end
While the truly great attain greatness
By doing what they are born to do
With or without the right name or title
Which are nothing but a tag.

24

This Life

Be not wise in your eyes
For nothing you are or have is from you
Not even the life you have
Nor the breath that keeps you alive
So be not proud or conceited

Wealth is far greater than riches
Essential things in life, money cannot buy
Like health, happiness, joy and peace
Or true friends and faithful family
So treasure wealth than riches

Life is full of ups and downs
Challenges here and difficulties there
These are not misfortunes
But building blocks of life
So we can live and not merely exist

Don't envy those who arrive before you
Because you have no idea of the roads
They've had to travel to arrive
But instead be motivated by them
So you can journey on till you arrive

Don't get carried away when you arrive
But remember the roads you've travelled
And don't despise those you overtake
They may end up higher than you
Because no one can be sure of tomorrow.

25

Living Or Existing

To be alive is not to live
But to merely exist
Life is for a purpose
Living is the pursuit of the purpose of life

A life of fame and fortune
But bereft of purpose
Is a mere existence
Leaving us empty and unfulfilled in the end

Are you living or existing?
Aspire to live
Before you expire
So you don't die without having lived.

26

Life A Journey

Life is a journey and not a destination
Enjoy the experience and adventure
Life is a one-way street
With no option to reverse or U-turn

If you're just starting off enjoy the excitement
If you're are almost at the end enjoy the sober reflections
If your road is smooth enjoy the ease
If rough and bumpy enjoy the difficulty

If you're in the driving seat enjoy the control
If you're being driven enjoy the dependency
If you're on a freeway enjoy the thrill
If you hit a deadlock enjoy the wait

If you've got a Ferrari enjoy the rarity
If yours is a jalopy enjoy the antiquity
If you've got company enjoy the fellowship
If you're travelling alone enjoy the solitude

Life is a journey and not a destination
Enjoy the experience and adventure
Life is a one-way street
With no option to reverse or U-turn

Once commenced we couldn't pause and re-start
Moments once passed could never be re-lived
Opportunities once missed could never be regained
Life progressed forward but never backwards

Therefore, let us enjoy every moment as they come
Whether we consider them good or bad
Because each moment is significant and relevant
In collectively shaping the quality of our experiences.

27

Life A Warfare

Life is warfare not a funfair!
By pushing and kicking we emerge from the womb
Into a life of struggle
By twisting and turning we depart from the world
To face the unknown

Life is warfare not a funfair!
Silent battles and raucous wars, visible and invisible
But none is spared
Demons we face and Angels unseen watching over us
But the struggle is real

Life is a warfare not a funfair!
Some fights we run to, others we run from
But fight we must fight on
Some fights we know and others we know nothing about
But the war rages on

Life is a warfare not a funfair!
We must fight with everything in us
Till we win
Running away in hope of living to fight another day
Leaves us living to fight another way.

2 8

Toolbox Of Life

In the toolbox of life are many tools
Each suited for particular functions
Although we are not availed of all the tools at all times
We would never be left without a tool at all
Leaving it up to us to use what we have as best as we can

In the toolbox of life are many tools
The tools we desire for a job
May not be the one life makes available to us
But if we waited for the tool we wanted
The job on hand may be left undone

In the toolbox of life are many tools
The tools made available to us
May not always be the ones we prefer
But could be used to fashion the tools we need
To get done the job that must be done

In the toolbox of life are many tools
The tools we sometimes are given
May not be right for the main job
But is right and needed for the job
Which must first be done before the main job

In the toolbox of life are many tools
Rightly using the tools available to us
In doing what has to be done with them
Eventually avails of every tool in the box
So we can do everything we are supposed to do.

29

Lessons Of Life

Life has taught me many lessons
Life has taught me dos and don'ts
Life has taught me that there is no
Problem without a solution
Question without an answer
Prison without a gate
Or lock without a key

Life has taught me many lessons
Life has taught me dos and don'ts
Life has taught me that there is no
Night without a day
Storm without a calm
Cloud without a sun
Or beginning without an end

Life has taught me many lessons
Life has taught me dos and don'ts
Life has taught me that there is
Always a way out of every situation
So instead of worrying and stressing
Let us seek and find that way
And walk in it till we are out.

30

Opportunity

Opportunity knocks but once
Knock, knock it whispers
While some people without hesitation open the door
Letting opportunity in and seize it
Others pause and consider before opening the door
By what time opportunity is gone

Opportunity comes to everyone
But not everyone welcomes it
While some people may be too occupied
Other people may simply not be interested
But those who miss the opportunity
Do so because they did not recognise the chance

Mathematically, if O stands for opportunity
It is absent in Yesterday
But present once in Today
And thrice in Tomorrow
But since tomorrow is not promised
Opportunity is only available today

Today's opportunity, though, will be gone tomorrow
Because tomorrow, today becomes yesterday
Banking on the triple chance in tomorrow is risky
Because, as today becomes yesterday tomorrow
So will tomorrow become today tomorrow
Leaving us with only one chance of opportunity
Which is available once only today.

31

Sunset At Dawn?

To everything there is a season
A time to be born and a time to die
A time for Winter and a time for Spring
A time for Summer and a time for Autumn
A time to plant and a time to pluck
But this time cannot be hurried

To every life there's a set time
A time to be conceived and a time to be born
A time in which to live and a time to die
And a time for everything in between
A time for every purpose in every moment
A time to be slow and not to hurry

Dawn to dusk the earth goes round and round
Moonlight! When it encounters the moon
And onward and around it goes round and round
Sunrise! When it meets with the sun
Onward it goes till goodbye it says to the sun
And it's sunset!

We cannot hurry the sun to rise at dusk
Nor can we make it to set at dawn
Because we cannot speed up or slow the earth
As we cannot alter our set time
Because time takes orders from no one
But the Author of Time, God the Creator.

3²

The Present

The past can't be changed
Learn from it and move on
The future is uncertain
Plan for it but don't chase it
The present is all we have
Don't waste it on the other two

When two forces collide
A more powerful force is formed
When the past collides with the future
The result is the present
The present is most powerful
Because now is the only thing we have

The present is a present
An irreplaceable precious gift
Which we must appreciate
It is all we can count on
And it doesn't last forever
But in a moment is gone forever.

33

Lemons For Lemonade

When life gives you lemons make lemonade
We embrace optimism to encourage us
But what if lemonade isn't what we need?
Do we still make lemonade for the sake of it?

Making lemonade when life gives us lemons
When we neither need nor drink lemonade
Will leave us stuck with lemonade
Which might eventually be poured down the drain

When life gives us lemons we make lemonade
So as not to waste our lemons
But only if we need or drink lemonade
Or else a wasted lemonade is wasted lemons

When life gives you lemons don't make lemonade
When you neither drink nor need lemonade
Except your lemonade if for those who need it
Or else you can pass the lemons on

When life gives us lemons and we pass them on
We will eventually receive the fruits we need
When life gives other people fruits they don't need
And they also pass them on.

34

Suicide By Murder

They believed they're indispensable
"My way or your end," they cooed
They behaved without restraint
"I hold the four aces," they exulted
They spoke with callous recklessness
Words too heavy to print

They believed we would drop dead
If they withdrew from us their help
Which they believed was our life support
But when they pulled the plug
They died when we stopped breathing
And we live to tell their story

The help we give to others in need
Is more beneficial to us than to them
Those we believe desperately need us
Are often the people we need the most
This is another of life's many ironies
That we could all learn from.

35

Not Missed Till Gone

Many things in life we take for granted
Because they're there when we need them
Only to miss them when they're gone
When we then realise their value
But only because they're now gone

We only miss the sun when it is dark
We only miss the rain when it is dry
We only miss childhood when we're grown
We only miss people when they're gone
But only because we feel alone

We should appreciate what we have
When we still have
We should enjoy the moments
Or we may miss out on life
But we see it cause it's now gone.

36

Unlearn

Once we've seen a thing
Once we've heard a thing
Once we've said a thing
Once we've tasted a thing
Once we've felt a thing
We cannot undo it

What we've learnt from what we saw
What we've learnt from what we heard
What we've learnt from what we said
What we've learnt from what we tasted
What we've learnt from what we felt
We can undo by unlearning.

37

Change

Change is the only constant
Because it does not change
Change happens every time
But does not just happen

Change only happens
When we act for change
Because nothing changes
If we change nothing

Change results in change
So change for change
Be the change you desire
And see things change.

38

Change The System

Everyone blames the system
For problems in the world
And perhaps rightly so
Because the world is ruled by the system

Everyone blames the system
For injustice in the world
Who is the system?
But the invisible product of our collective design

Everyone blames the system
For the state of the world
But we are the system
So let us change the system and heal the world.

Speaking Frankly

SPEAKING FRANKLY

39

Fitly-Spoken

"Hey! What did I hear you say?"
Words are so tender yet so powerful
Words are so weightless yet so heavy
Words are intangible yet
Words result in tangible consequences

Harsh words spoken and lives are broken
Kind words spoken and lives are mended
Every word spoken initiates a creation
From raw material to word-in-progress
Till its mission is accomplished

With words we can build or destroy
With words we can comfort or distress
With words we can inspire or despair
With words we can unite or divide
Words are building blocks

We are artists painting with words
We should speak skilfully and prudently
By speaking only when necessary
And only what is necessary
So as to produce a masterpiece.

40

Doing And Saying

Doing and saying are two different things
Some things we say but don't do
And some things we do but don't say
Between the things we say and do
The things we do speak the loudest

Doing and saying are two different things
The things we say reflect what we know
While the things we do reveal who we are
Between what we know and who we are
Who we are speaks the loudest

Doing and saying are two different things
The things we say are intangible expressions
While the things we do are tangible evidence
Between the things we say and do
Our actions speak the loudest

Doing and saying are two different things
The things we do will amount to nothing
If our doings are not as our sayings
Because between our doings and sayings
The things we do matter the most.

41

Walk The Talk

Some people like to talk
About the things they know are popular
Although they may not truly believe
And so they do not walk their talk

Some people like to talk
About the things they openly condemn
Although they may secretly indulge in
And so they do not walk their talk

Some people like to talk
They talk and talk all the time
But because they don't walk their talk
They end up having to talk a lot.

42

Teaching By Example

We ought to learn more than we teach
Because by learning we know more
And by knowing more we can teach more
Teaching is best by example

We ought to learn more than we teach
Because by learning we are able to do
And by doing we are able teach more
Teaching is best by example

We ought to learn more than we teach
Because good learners become better doers
And better doers become better teachers
Teaching is best by example.

43

Rhapsody

Everyone wants to know the truth
But those willing to accept it are few
Because the truth is bitter
And usually very costly

Every man proclaims his goodness
But a faithful man is hard to find
Because talk is cheap
And easier said than done

Every woman wants to be loved
But most get hurt and heartbroken
Because love is blind
And cannot be trusted

44

Without Love

Love is the salt of life
It brings out its true taste
Love is the light of life
It reveals its radiant beauty
Love is the meaning of life
To love is to live and to live is to love

Good becomes bad if love is absent
Acceptance becomes tolerance
Correction becomes condemnation
Disciplining becomes punishment
Charity becomes an investment
Good deeds mean nothing if not done in love

No good is present if love is absent
Charity becomes self-glorification
Kindness becomes cruelty
Good intentions become evil deeds
Better is a little done in love
Than a lot done without love.

45

Friendship

Friendship is the bedrock of lasting relationship
Relationships are best when founded on friendship
Best friends make happy marriages
Best friends make trusting business partners
Best friends make best mates

Relationships which start as friendship thrive more
Otherwise uncertainties are inevitable
And those involved may never become friends
With friendship absent, relationships are precarious
And are likely to end worse than they began

Therefore, before we become anything else
Let us first become friends
Then we stand a better chance of making the most
Of whatever else we desire to become
Be it spouses, partners, associates or buddies.

46

Men Are From Mars

Men and women are both humans
And have the same and single origin
But whereas men are from Mars
Women on the other hand are from Venus
Thus the origin of the conundrum

The conundrum of the misunderstanding
That exists between men and women
In words, feeling, and comprehension
Which has set men apart from women
Plunging both into an endless war

A universal war of the planets
Between fictional Martians and Venusians
Because where Venusians feel Martians see
And when Venusians speak Martians are lost
In a language they thought they understood

Not understanding, men blame women for nagging
Who in turn blame men for failing to listen
Men should therefore not assume but seek clarity
And women should speak for men to understand
So we can end this war and conundrum.

47

The Wise Gambler

The prudent tries to get a dollar's worth out of a dollar
The thrifty tries to get a dollar's worth out of a cent
The shrewd tries to make a dollar out of a cent
But the gambler tries to make a cent out of many dollars

The gambler believes very much in his own wisdom
So he throws in a cent hoping to win many dollars
He loses but is wise enough not to let go of a cent
So he throws in a dollar hoping to recoup the lost cent

The dollar is lost as was the cent but does he quit?
I cannot lose a dollar and a cent, he assures himself
The jackpot is mine to win, he believes
So the wise gambler throws in even more dollars.

He gambles and gambles gambling on
Till he's down to his last cent and out
But does he lick his wound and quit?
No, he borrows, begs, or steals to gamble on

The gambler believes in his shrewd wisdom
Not knowing that gambling is the game of fools
Where you give all in exchange for nothing
A deal only a fool will take.

48

Foolish Ignorance

Is foolishness the same thing as ignorance?
Does ignorance make us foolish, for instance
Or are we ignorant because of foolishness?
For an answer I went on a long walk

On my way I bumped into the two
And discovered both to be best of friends
Although not related by blood
Because both are strikingly dissimilar

When I saw foolishness buy something useless
And ignorance refuse to buy something useful
Only because he was ignorant of its usefulness
I knew I had found the answer I sought.

49

Blissful Ignorance

Ignorance is bliss, they say
It is blissful not to know
What we ought not to know
But fatal not to know
What we ought to know

Ignorance and knowledge
Are like two non-identical twins
Where one dwells the other is not far off
Because the more we know
Is the more we don't know

Knowledge is deep
But ignorance is deeper
While we may know and fail to do
We could never do that
Which we are ignorant of

Ignorance is ubiquitous
It abounds where knowledge abounds
And abounds where knowledge is lacking
The educated and uneducated are both ignorant
For each thing we know
there are more things we don't know

Ignorance rests comfortably
In the bosom of kings
And in the cradle of beggars
It kisses the lips of princes
And massages the thighs of paupers

Ignorance is bliss
Because if we knew everything
We would be tormented to the grave
With the pain and burden of knowing
Wishing we were ignorant of some things.

50

Arrogant Ignorance

Arrogant arrogance struts in confidence
Confidence in her imperious superiority
Superiority founded in simple ignorance
Ignorance puffed up by arrogant arrogance

Arrogant arrogance struts in confidence
Blissfully unaware of simple ignorance
That makes her imperiously superior
Which although she isn't but only arrogant

Arrogant arrogance strutting in confidence
Stumbled and fell tripped by incompetence
Which exposed her gaping inconsequence
Making her realise she was simply ignorant.

51

Anger

Anger rests calmly in the bosom of the foolish
A faithful companion of those who refuse to learn
Despite the regret and sorrow constant with its presence
After its bidding they have dutifully obeyed

Anger walks confidently by the side of the foolish
Urging them to speak and do things better avoided
Because of the hurt and pain that is bound to follow
After such deeds have finally been done

Anger quickly abandons the company of the foolish
After much havoc and destruction, it has wrecked
Leaving them to suffer the consequences alone
A true friend in deed but not in need.

5²

Foolish Pride

Foolish pride makes foolish the proud
Who but in themselves alone believe
Are better and wiser than the rest
Who up to them alone must look

Foolish pride makes empty the proud
Who nestled in their inflated ego
Estrange themselves from the rest
Leaving them unwanted and alone

Foolish pride is simply foolishness
We are all unique and different
And none is better than the rest
So only the foolish can be proud.

53

A Fool

He who does not know
And does not know
That he does not know
Is a fool

He who does not know
And thinks he knows
But does not know
Is a fool

Is he who knows
But does not know
That he knows
Still a fool?

54

Knowledge

Knowledge is power, they say
But only when rightly applied
Because to know and not do
Is not different to not knowing

Knowledge is deep, they say
But not deeper than ignorance
Both have no limits or boundaries
Nor any beginning or ending

Knowledge is humbling, I say
Because the more we know
Is the more we know that
There's more we don't know

Knowledge is a burden, I say
Because the more we know is
The more we wished we didn't know
But it is better to know than not to know.

55

What They Said

Every day is for the thief, one day is for the owner
What day is for the owner, if every day is for the thief?
The patient dog eats the fattest bone
Did the impatient dog eat the meat?

Slow and steady wins the race
Even in a short distance race?
Cut your coat according to your cloth
Even if your cloth is not enough for your size?

A penny saved is a penny earned
Don't we have to first earn a penny before saving it?
Good things come to those who wait
Even if we did nothing while waiting?

56

Falling High

Every fall is gradual
We don't hit rock-bottom instantly
We first drop a notch
Soon as we are getting used to the new low
Another drop

Every fall is different
We drop in different ways each time
But downwards we go
When we think it couldn't get any worse
Another drop

Every fall is gradual
Down and lower we go
Till rock-bottom we reach
Then the only way is up
The rise

Every fall is a thrill
We fall in order to rise
Above our previous height
Where the fall began
Higher we rise.

57

Higher We Rise

We fail and fall in life
Sometimes by accident or mistake
And other times by own carelessness
But we fall to rise again

We rise and learn in life
Becoming, stronger, better and wiser
Able to advance further and wider
And higher than before

Higher we rise in life
After we fail and take a fall
Because in falling we learn and grow
Becoming more than we were.

Musings

MUSINGS

58

The Burly Twins And The Little Girl

There was an old man who once lived in a remote village many years ago. It so happened that in the same village also lived two young burly twins whose notoriety spread beyond the village to distant neighbouring towns as well. Although the twins were practically inseparable, they weren't quite identical even though both shared some similar traits. The burly twins displayed negative characteristics and were bullies that terrorised anyone they met especially those who unwittingly indulged them. They were particularly fond of assaulting the old man, who was affectionately known as "Oldie" within the village. They twisted this name by taunting the helpless old man who was an easy prey because he didn't seem to know how to silence the twins nor stop their tormenting of him. Oftentimes the two mischievous boys would bang loudly on Oldie's door for no reason other than to alarm him, and once he opened his door to check who it was, the twins would burst out in laughter while sneering and jeering at him as though he was a foolish old man. Initially, Oldie found this

behaviour mildly irritating but as it persisted it began to deeply
disturb him to the point of causing him distress and depressing him.
But this dear man, affectionately known by the villagers, found himself
helpless as he was hapless, because he simply didn't have a clue on how
to deal with the annoying, irritating and trouble-some two.

In the same village, also lived a beautiful and quick-witted young
girl who considered herself a good friend of Oldie's. She occasionally
visited the old man to keep him company, help run a few errands while
also doing some chores within the house. On that particular day, as the
young girl opened the door to Oldie's house, she found him sitting
looking sorrowful and afflicted. Moved by compassion and concern,
she persuaded Oldie to confide in her about what was troubling his
mind. With some hesitation and feeling ashamed, the old man revealed
he needed help and so he told her about the terrible twins. As fate
would have it, just as Oldie recounted his woes to the young girl
brought about by the actions of the burly twins, they struck again! A
loud bang at the door startled the pair as they sat and talked, visibly
shaken, the old man motioned towards the door. But quick as a flash,
the young girl told him to sit back so she could answer the door. No
sooner had she opened the door when the twins froze at the
unexpected sight, barely knowing how to respond, they instantly
ran from the house as quickly as their legs could carry them. On
hearing the commotion, the old man stepped outside, looked
around at the running boys, unable to figure out what had transpired.
Once they sat back down, the young girl sauntered into the lounge
smiling victoriously as she shared with him what had happened. She
went on to assure him that now that the twins were aware of their
friendship, they would never bother him again. And truly, the burly
bully twins never bothered Oldie again as long as he remained friends
with that young village girl.

The burly twins represent Worry and Fear, and the young girl is Faith while the old man represents you and I. To overcome the threat posed by worry and fear we need faith. Faith is defined as complete trust or confidence in something or someone, and in the context of the story represents complete trust in God first and foremost but also a belief in oneself or self-confidence. Note, however, that faith in oneself which isn't founded on faith in God is in vain. On the other hand, faith in God would naturally empower us with self-confidence thus enabling us to do things which ordinarily we couldn't do on our own.

Musing

There's a saying to the effect that when fear knocks you get faith to answer the door. Without faith it is impossible to live a wholesome life, a life where we are in perfect control of our emotions such that instead of being overcome by negative emotions like worry, anxiety, fear, anger, distress, sadness, and depression, we rise above them. It is impossible that we could pass through life without encountering situations which evoke negative emotions. Therefore, in order to maintain a positive disposition in spite of circumstances, we need supernatural help which only God can avail us of. It is also impossible to relate with, please, or obtain anything from God if we don't have faith in God. Therefore, in order to obtain the help we need to overcome the pressures and stresses of life, we need to have faith in God. Faith ensures that we victor over every circumstance instead of becoming victims. Keep the faith and let her get the door whenever the bullies come banging on your door.
Could you be a victim of faithlessness?

59

The Mountain In Labour

One day, people noticed a great commotion around a mountain; huge smoke was being emitted from its top, the earth around it quaked vigorously such that every nearby tree fell and crashed while rocks were loosened as they tumbled down, with the resulting noise of groaning like a woman in painful labour. The mountain seemed to be giving birth to something as it continued to shudder furiously attracting attention as more and more people gathered at the base of the mountain to witness what would be reproduced. The people were excited and expectant and everyone was certain that the mountain would birth something huge, because of the associated noise and commotion it produced. Eventually, the long-awaited time came as a huge gap appeared in the side of the mountain followed by a brief moment were nothing seemed to happen at all. Finally, the tiny head of a mouse poked out from the gap before it came running out and away from the spectators. Alas, the mountain after all that commotion had birthed not something big as expected but instead a tiny mouse. The people were aghast, incredulous, and disappointed at the result.

Aesop's fable *The Mountain in Labour* has been retold several times over several historical periods and have been given a variety of interpretations and applications, usually politically. The moral of the story resonates with some popular sayings, such as, "much ado about nothing," "empty vessels make the most noise," and also, the relatively modern "too much hype kills the vibe." In whatever we do in life, it is better that we surprise people by exceeding their expectations of us instead of falling short of what was expected. When we go on and on about something we're doing or are going to do, we build up expectation which we might fail to meet eventually. But, when we say little and instead focus on doing more than talking we exceed expectations. In this social media age where many people advertise their private lives publicly, including sharing with the world on Facebook and Instagram details of their lives that are best kept private, it is so easy to get caught up in the trend and hype about our projects, visions, or dreams. An additional danger here, apart from exposing ourselves to avoidable and unwanted criticism, opposition, and discouragement, is that we could be tempted to spend more of our time in creating a buzz around what we intend to do such that we are left with little time to actually get something done. It is better to work in silence and let our achievements do the talking for us. It is better to focus on doing what is needful than talking about it, so that our result will speak for itself.

Musing

Don't let your hype kill your vibe. Talk less but do more so that you always exceed people's expectations of you. It is not what we intend to do that counts but instead what we have done. Efforts don't mean much if not backed with commensurate results; result is everything. Focus on achieving the best results in each situation so that your achievement makes the noise on your behalf, instead of hyping your efforts before the results are realised.

Could you be killing your vibe with your hype?

60

The Eagle, Sheep, and Hen

Many years ago, the eagle sent her son out into the forest to hunt for food for the family. After flying around for several hours he found no prey in sight, so the young eagle decided to venture further to new territories and as a result flew to the part of the village inhabited by humans. From high above in the sky, he saw a lone lamb grazing in the green field with the mother sheep a few yards away, and immediately it swooped down grabbing the unsuspecting lamb on both sides with its strong talons before quickly ascending back into the sky. The mother sheep saw what had happened but said nothing. When the eagle returned to the family nest with its impressive catch, the mother eagle was excited but, before settling down to the process of dismembering the lamb for dinner, asked the young eagle whether or not the lamb's mother saw it take away her lamb. The young eagle replied that yes, the mother sheep had seen it grab the lamb. The mother eagle then asked what the mother sheep did in response to which the young eagle replied, "nothing." The mother eagle, troubled and deep in thought, asked the young eagle to return the lamb where it was snatched from and to look for another prey.

Surprised and confused, the young eagle obeyed. While descending to the spot where it had grabbed the lamb earlier, it sighted some chicks flocking nearby led by their mother hen. So, as soon as it dropped the lamb it quickly pounced on one of the chicks and fled. The mother hen chased after it cursing and clucking loudly while threatening hell and brimstone on the young eagle. When the young eagle arrived home, the same question was asked about the reaction of the mother, when he responded that the mother hen had chased after with cursing and threats, the mother eagle informed the young eagle that it should henceforth hunt chicks but never lambs. Inquisitive about the new instructions, the young eagle asked why and the mother eagle explained. The mother hen had demonstrated all that she could do, which was no threat at all to them, but that what the mother sheep would do remained a mystery since she didn't say or do anything after her baby lamb was snatched. The silence of the sheep represented more threat than the loud empty rantings of the hen.

Musing

Silence is golden, they say. When faced with intense provocation or severe threat, peaceful quietness is a great strength in more ways than one. Remaining calm helps us to get the right perspective on the matter thus making it possible for us to properly appraise the situation so that we could then arrive at a definitive and effective solution. Similarly, when the threat, provocation, or opposition is from an individual or people, refusing to reveal our thoughts or intentions empowers us over the opponent because they are unsure of what we would do in response. Not knowing our thoughts, intentions, or possible action disarms the opponent who wouldn't know whether to attack or defend, or how to. Silence in response to provocation, or peaceful quietness in the midst of a storm, makes us look stronger than we truly are and thus a bigger threat than we might be.

Could you be a victim of your own making?

61

The Deer And The King

There was once a king who ruled over a vast kingdom and who liked to feast on deer. He commissioned the best hunters in his kingdom on a special assignment to hunt for the choicest bucks, stags or venison they could find. These were then kept in a large confinement from where each deer was selected and prepared for the king's dining pleasure. One day, it was the turn of a doe who had recently had a new baby to be eaten but she pleaded with the king to kindly spare her life until she had completed nursing her new-born. The king agreed and ordered for the next deer in line to be killed and prepared, but when the doe was taken back to the pen and she realised that another young deer would be killed in her place, she was deeply moved to sadness. She couldn't come to terms with the idea that another deer's baby would be killed in order for her to raise her own baby. So she returned to the king and requested that she be killed instead as was originally intended, further explaining that she couldn't bear the thought of another deer's baby dying in order for the benefit of her own baby.

This show of kindness, empathy and selflessness deeply touched the king who as a result decided not to feast on deer anymore but instead ordered that all the captive deer be released into the wild immediately.

The king also ordered that henceforth no hunter in his vast kingdom should hunt deer whilst imposing a death penalty for offenders. This ancient fable reveals the power of kindness and empathy. It demonstrates how a little act of kindness could significantly impact our world positively. In a world where equity and justice are rare, empathy is what is needed to turn things around for everyone. We live in a world where some people benefit at the expense of others, where a particular group of people are deliberately marginalised and restrained so that another group of people would be privileged, where a social class comprised of a minority profit from the majority lower classes thus leaving them impoverished, and where particular groups of people are dominated and exploited by other groups which are stronger, physically or otherwise. We live in a world where the privileged deer population do not only relish their self-entitled position but are also willing to do anything possible to ensure that their privilege is not tampered with, even though unjustly acquired. The entire deer population of our world could be free if some of the privileged deer show a little kindness and empathy, thus making the world a better place where equity and justice prevail.

Musing

The privilege you enjoy is not quite beneficial if it comes at the expense of a fellow human, because there is a price you pay eventually. A privilege, for instance, which leaves you feeling insecure, because you don't know what the people based on whose restriction you are privileged will do or when they may act, is not quite an advantage but a disadvantage and a burden. Also, openly condemning a situation while continuing to enjoy what perks it offer is to indulge in hypocrisy and deception (including of self). The deer in the story didn't only empathise but she acted on her empathy by giving up her privilege in an act of self-sacrifice. Until we are willing to sacrifice our privileges for the benefit of those based on whose disadvantage we are privileged, our words and activism would remain an exercise in futility.

Could your privilege be denying someone else or a people their natural rights?

62

The Sun And The
North Wind

The sun and the north wind once argued about who was stronger and since none was willing to concede to the other, both agreed upon a contest. A traveller wrapped in a heavy cloak happened to be passing by below the two of them at the same time. The sun and the north wind agreed that whoever was able to rid the travelling man of his coat was the stronger of the two. The north wind went first and blew its hardest with so much force that its lungs almost burst, but this made the travelling man to grip harder on his coat in order not to lose it. After several unsuccessful attempts the north wind disappointedly gave up trying. It was now the sun's turn and, instead of being forceful as the north wind, it gently warmed up the weather with a charming smile. As the sun increased its warmth it didn't take long for the travelling man to look back grinning at the sun while casually removing his cloak which he flung away. The contest was quickly over, to the amazement of the north wind who only then conceded to the sun as the stronger of the two.

The foregoing is an adaptation of Aesop's fable *The North Wind and the Sun* which teaches the superiority of gentle persuasion over brutal force. Force is naturally met with resistance, which was the traveller's response to the north wind. Force is also usually met with force resulting in aggression and violence. Persuasion, on the other hand, is naturally met with acceptance and cooperation as did the traveller to the sun. People are more inclined to do something when they believe that the decision is purely theirs and not one imposed on them. Persuasion is a powerful and effective strategy in every sphere of life including, personal and corporate relationships, politics and commerce, sales and marketing, dispute resolution, and arbitration. Persuasion doesn't mind adopting the "stooping to conquer mentality" to achieve its desired end. Persuasion, however, must never be mis-applied for the purpose of deception or manipulation because doing such would be immoral and criminal. Moreover, such misapplication of persuasion invariably becomes counterproductive eventually when victims finally realise they had been deceived. Nonetheless, adopting persuasion instead of force is altogether more rewarding.

Musing

Force might look impressive but it is actually weaker in comparison to persuasion because the latter succeeds over and over where the former fails repeatedly. Persuasion could prove very useful in family relationships includ-ing between spouses and between parents and their children. The most effective way of ensuring performance or change in behaviour is by letting the other person chose to do what is needed on their own volition. When people believe that their actions are largely their own making then they are more likely to implement such actions to their best ability and for a long term with-out requiring constant supervision or monitoring. When people feel empowered with choice they do better whatever they've chosen to do.
Could you be applying force where only persuasion will bring results?

63

The Potter And The Clay

An old wise man went to a potter's workshop one day to observe the potter do his work. As he sat quietly in a corner he carefully watched the potter pick up a huge pile of clay from the floor and place it on the work table before meticulously picking out tiny stones and objects from the clay. He then kneaded it gently to rid it of air bubbles. The old man observed the potter place the prepared clay on the wheel as he got ready to start moulding. Overcome with curiosity, he asked the potter, "Do you already have an object in mind or does the wheel and clay determine the final object?" The potter amused by the question replied, "Before I collect the clay, I already know what object I want to form. The object determines the pottery process and not the other way round." The potter went on to elaborate that the final product determined the quantity and texture of the clay used, the intensity of the heat it was passed through and for how long, and also type of decorative finishing applied. The old man thanked the potter and left the workshop deep in thought.

We are all clay in the potter's hands, the potter in this case representing God our creator. Before forming us in the womb God already knew whom we were meant to be and also why we are created. Our identity and purpose determines what goes into our constitution and design, as well as the circumstances we encounter in life. To get the best out of life we need to realise our true identities which in turn would enable us to also uncover our respective purposes, and then live in accordance to both. Just as the clay cannot and doesn't decide what object is formed by the potter, we also are in no position to decide our identity and purpose. God alone does. It means then that our dreams and ambitions in life would also have to be inspired by or aligned to our identity and purpose if we are to experience fulfilment in the end. Incidentally, the society we live in presents a formidable challenge and obstacle against our true identity and purpose by offering us various other alternatives in this regard. We are faced with so much societal and peer pressure which tend to make us conform to general norms and standards while denying our individual uniqueness with respect to identity and purpose. For instance, many people aspire for financial wealth in pursuance of success in life but only because the societal concept of success has more to do with abundance of money than fulfilment of purpose. The perspective of the society tends to suggest that we all have the same purpose in life, and which is to accumulate enough money to satisfy every of our desires. Note, however, that the society isn't the potter who made us. God is the potter and He had a plan for us before causing us to be born.

As the wise old man departed from the potter's workshop his thoughts centred on whether the clay could require the potter to make it into a particular object. Or, having been made into an object, question the potter, "What is this you've made?"

Musing

What would be your reaction to a clay questioning the potter about the object he turned it into? Incredulous? Well, certain behaviours aren't that far from a clay questioning the potter about its final outcome. For instance, people who surgically enhance some physical features in order to look more beautiful. Or, those who attempt to change their gender either by cross-dressing or surgery. This is also the case when we reject our true identities in preference for whom the society prefers us to be. It is worth noting that the clay would've remained just a clay had the potter not selected it and transformed it into an object. Likewise, we owe our existence to God who caused us to be born. We should therefore be grateful to God, starting with acknowledging and appreciating what and why He made us.

Could you be questioning God about your making?

64

The Unhooded Monk

A social experiment was conducted some years back which somewhat resonates with the moral revealed by the biblical story of the Good Samaritan. A supposed victim of an assault lay beaten and battered by the roadside in blood-soaked clothing by a roadside near a train station. The objective of the experiment was to see who among the passers-by would make time out of their busy schedule to assist the victim. It was morning rush-hour and not one single person who walked past this man stopped to check on him let alone to assist him. Interestingly, among the passers-by were a priest, a medical doctor, a nurse, and a schoolteacher. Although the medical doctor and nurse took a second glance at the man, they nonetheless hurried along on a mission to catch their train. The priest and teacher barely glanced at the man directly but instead both kept looking straight ahead pretending not to have seen him.

The result was surprising to the researchers who conducted the experiment because they had expected the aforementioned categories of people would have behaved differently from the populace. This expectation is perhaps based on the assumption that our profession reflects our nature or personality. This assumption is, however, belied by these sayings, "The hood does not make the monk" and "The clothes do not make the man." Appearance can be deceitful and therefore must be avoided as a yardstick for determining a person's character. A person who usually dresses up in clean suit, tie, and fine shoes may be a lesser gentleman than the person who is often scruffily dressed in hoods, baggy pants, and trainers. A medical doctor could be more a serial killer than the truck driver who also belongs to a Harley Davidson motorbike gang. Likewise, a person who isn't religious could be more morally-inclined than the priest who is usually clad in a soutane. The point here is that a person's profession isn't the same as his personality, and that appearances do not always equate to behaviour. It is therefore wrong to judge a person's character based on appearance or profession. Sadly, some people have been wrongly arrested or convicted for crimes they didn't commit but only because of their appearance. On the other hand, some people have also been appointed to offices and jobs that they're ill-equipped for but, again, only because they looked the part.

We are what we do behaviourally and not the works that we do, and sometimes, our behaviour doesn't match our appearance. It is possible to be a monk without possessing or adorning a hood.

Musing

We might have at one time or another been victims of stereotyping, without even realising so. We may also have been culprits and have wrongly judged other people by their appearance including the colour of their skin. And, why so? Perhaps because we believed that the hood made the monk. On the other hand, we may also have failed to act upon our innate desires simply because we didn't feel qualified to do so, we didn't have the hood. But, with or without the hood we can still actualise our natural potentials and accomplish the things we were born to do. While the hood (in this case training and qualifications) enhances our abilities and skills, the potentials we are born with can still be engaged productively if we were not privileged to own a hood. We must avoid the temptation to bury our dreams and visions for lack of a hood. Remember, the hood does not make the monk.
Could you be burying your potentials for lack of a hood?

65

Chance Meet?

Some years ago I randomly bumped into an old friend on my way to the shop and we got talking. We no longer had each other's contact details, but it turned out he had been trying to get in touch with me for a project. He doesn't live in my neighbourhood and, according to him, he wasn't even sure what he was doing in the area because he was meant to be at the other side of town but had somehow gotten on a wrong bus and was now trying to get redirected when we bumped into each other. Well we exchanged phone numbers and eventually completed the project. Nothing in life is a coincidence.

Oftentimes, we attribute some unplanned or unexpected events to chance. We may bump into a complete stranger on our way to work, for instance, and regard the meeting as a random coincidence. Or we may find ourselves in a place we hadn't intentionally planned to be and believe that such happened by chance. Although some things may occur as though by mere chance, nothing ever really happens by chance. Instead, everything that comes to pass was meant to be¾they were preordained or predestined to be. And for specific reasons too. God allows paths to cross, when they do, for a reason.

Some people come into our lives to assist us, cause us to grow and develop, sometimes through hurtful and painful experiences, others come to accompany us through part of our journey, while other people come to connect us with other people who would help us in one way or another, but everyone comes for a reason or for a season. Likewise, different associations are purposed for different durations: While some meetings are intended for long-term associations or relationships, others are meant to be short-lived and last only for a while. Regardless of how a breakup occurs, it is important to ascertain whether the relationship had come to its natural end having served its purpose, so that we can let go of it instead of trying in vain to bring it back to life and make it work. A failed relationship could be an opportunity and a redirection to a new relationship. Letting go at the right time would ensure that we are prepared and ready to avail ourselves of new opportunities, which the past opportunities might've been intended to prepare us for.

Since the people we meet in life, some of whom become part of our lives for given periods, are not necessarily due to our personal determination or efforts, also, since we come into and lose contact with people, deliberately and unintentionally, and because we don't know in advance when will meet or be parted from them, it is rather expedient that we treat everyone we meet right, regardless of how we met them. We should treat everyone we meet with love, kindness and goodwill not necessarily for how they might've related with us but at least as a mark of gratitude to the all-knowing God who deemed it fit and necessary that our paths and theirs should cross in the first place. Be grateful for everyone you meet in life and be thankful for meeting them.

Musing

Life is like a train journey. Although we travel alone we meet people along our journey, and while some people travel longer with us others share the coach with us for a short while. We may find some people entertaining and others annoying, some fellow passengers may hurt or disappoint us while others may comfort and be nice to us, but everyone serves a useful purpose in our life. Although our focus should be on arriving at our destination, we must however ensure to enjoy the company of the other passengers while we still have their company, so as to make the most of our experience of the journey. Could you be unknowingly ungrateful for some people you crossed path with?

66

Love Is Not Blind

Our wrong understanding of what love truly is has led us to the assumption that love is blind. The popular saying, love is blind, could suggest that love (defined as an intense feeling of deep affection) blinds its victims to the realities of life thus compelling them to do things that they ordinarily wouldn't do. For instance, when a very beautiful girl chooses to marry a man who could not be said to be handsome nor is financially wealthy. Or when a rich handsome man decides to marry a poor uneducated girl who isn't physically attractive. Love in this instance is invariably associated with romance between a man and woman, which happens to be our most common understanding of the meaning of love.

Love, however, is more than a feeling, an emotion, but instead is a supernatural force that flows from God Who is described in the Bible as love (1 John 4: 8, 16). To better understand what love is we have to look as some of its key characteristics. First, love is unconditional and is not dependent on any factors or circumstances. It means that we love people not because we feel they are deserving of our love but simply because it is the right thing to do.

Also, love is not purposed for selfish interests but instead for the benefit of the recipient, which eventually would benefit the giver. Furthermore, love is not only spoken but is acted upon such that even without saying it our actions would clearly demonstrate our love. Love is pure, enduring, tolerant, considerate, moderate, understanding, forgiving, and kind.

Love is therefore not blind as we generally suppose but instead love sees very clearly while choosing to ignore those things popularly regarded as unacceptable or negative. Note, however, that love doesn't condone evil or wrong but hates and condemns them even though it doesn't hate or condemn those who do evil or wrong. Love accepts people as they are but will not accept their bad deeds. This unconditional nature of love could be responsible for its being misconstrued as blind.

Musing

Perhaps we could all be like love and refuse to judge or condemn other people for who they are or what they do while not condoning any wrongs done by them. We could see physical and other differences between different groups of people and yet choose to treat everyone equally, simply as human beings. We could choose to be kind to strangers as we are to friends and family. We should choose to love not because we cannot see but because we simply don't care.

Could you be partial with your love?

67

Criticism

Some years ago a close acquaintance of mine made what I believed to be a scathing remark about something I had written and shared online. A greater part of his criticism was misguided, perhaps because he had failed to comprehend my message while wrongly assuming that I was roundly condemning the particular religion, Christianity, he was subscribed to even though he knew that I also practiced the same religion. His erroneous assumption nonetheless, his criticism wasn't entirely unfounded because his remark about my using the word "most" in a statement I had made, which with the benefit of hindsight I later realised bothered on generalisation, instead of "some" or "many" since I couldn't back my "most" with verifiable statistics, was valid.

Although I was initially offended by the tone and content of his critical remarks, I didn't fail to learn something from the part of his criticism I found to be valid, which improved my writing. From then on I became more careful with my choice of words so as not to wrongly generalise thereby tarring an entire population with the same brush based only on a part of the population, even if they represented a significant proportion. I later told the person in question what I had thought of his criticism and after some explanations from both sides the issue was resolved while the lesson I had learnt previously remained with me, and to my benefit.

Not many people are able to handle criticism as well as they appreciate compliments. We all like our efforts to be appreciated but when our efforts are faulted, rightly or wrongly, or perceived mistakes highlighted, the common reaction is not always positive or welcoming. Experience has, however, taught me that criticism can be beneficial even when not objectively-driven. Objective criticism is positive because it helps to constructively highlight areas where genuine improvement is needed. Since none is perfect we all have need and room for improvement. Non-constructive criticism on the other hand, although not objectively-driven, can also be beneficial when we demonstrate some degree of maturity. Such criticisms although usually underlain by negative sentiments (e.g., envy, jealousy, bitterness, dislike, or hate) are also often subtly revealing. A curt remark could be masking secret admiration, a personal attack could be a veiled recognition of the victim's potentials or skills, while a criticism which focuses only a small aspect of the entire work could be an indication that the greater part of the work couldn't be faulted. Constructive or non-constructive, we can turn every criticism to our advantage instead of allowing ourselves to become discouraged as a result.

Musing

A piece of information is to be accepted if it is authentic and thus valid. But then even a piece of false or wrong information could still serve a useful purpose. First, it could help highlight what is right and true. Also, it could serve as a warning or deterrent preventing us from doing what isn't right. So also is criticism. A fact-based criticism presented constructively should inspire us to do better while a non-constructive criticism could also inspire us to do better by challenging us to do more than we've done presently. Even a misguided criticism driven by petty sentiments can also be harnessed to our advantage when we are determined to succeed against all odds. We should therefore embrace criticism positively for the purpose of allowing it to challenge instead of discourage us.

Could you be missing out on the benefit of criticism?

68

Sorry, Thank You

To be sorry is to feel regretful or penitent about something we've done which we subsequently acknowledged was wrong or inappropriate. It means then that before we say sorry to someone we had wronged or offended, we must first be sure that we are penitent and truly regret what we had done. And if we are truly sorry, we are more likely to do whatever we can to avoid repeating the same offence. Otherwise, saying sorry would amount to abuse or misuse of the term. Going by what commonly obtains in human interactions, it would seem that some people use the word "sorry" lightly without really meaning it. It is common for some people to simply say sorry just so as to avoid a conversation which could prove uncomfortable to them, perhaps because some of their character flaws would be highlighted in the process, even though they don't believe that they've done anything wrong. Or they could do so to prevent an argument while not truly being sorry.

When we use sorry wrongly it does more harm than good. First, we say what we don't mean, which is a form of deception.

Also, when we go on repeating the same offence for which we've said sorry several times it doesn't speak well of us and it makes our sorry worthless. Additionally, people may find it difficult believing us when we say we're sorry. More importantly, saying sorry dismissively denies us the opportunity of assessing our actions in order to learn, change, grow and develop. Consequently, it is advisable to only say sorry when we're truly sorry and, more importantly, when we're willing to make the much-needed change so as not to repeat the things we said sorry for.

Like sorry, "Thank you" is also often underused or misused and, again, for the wrong reasons. Sometimes we neglect to thank people for their good deeds or kindness perhaps because we feel entitled, especially when those involved are close friends or family members. Other times, also, we use thank you casually such that it fails to convey a true and deep sense of gratitude or appreciation, which is what thank you is purposed for. Worse still is when we use thank you curtly or sarcastically to mask our displeasure at how someone has treated us.

While this application of thank you could represent courtesy or politeness, or it might help diffuse a potential conflict, it could also be unhealthy if we stifled our feelings instead of expressing them for the purpose of dealing with the unpleasant situation.

It is important that we acknowledge kindness and other good deeds no matter how little or insignificant by expressing our appreciation and gratitude, because not only is the right thing to do it also encourages the doer by making them feel appreciated. It is equally important that we don't misuse thank you in any way and for any reason so that we don't convey a wrong message to the other person.

Musing
The world would be a better place and our lives easier when we mean what we say and say what we mean. Being truly sorry before we say we are sorry ensures that we may not have to say sorry again for the very same thing, because if we are truly sorry we would endeavour to make amends such that we don't repeat the same offences. Being thankful is a virtue which should be cultivated because when we appreciate people for their good deeds we inspire them to do more. Also, when we are truly grateful for the things we've received we are more likely to value them more, meaning that we would derive more satisfaction from them also.
Could you be misusing sorry and thank you?

69

Dualism

Every coin has two sides as there are two sides to every story involving two people. Life is the absence of death as death is the absence of life; night is on the other side of day as joy is on the flip side of sadness; goodness exists because of badness or else it wouldn't be recognisable. Opposites or contrasts enhance the meaning of each other and thus our appreciation of each. If we didn't die we probably wouldn't appreciate life as much as we did, but the existence of death and our awareness of it helps us cherish life. Likewise, if evil didn't exist we wouldn't understand the true worth of goodness, which we could then easily take for granted. Light exists only because darkness also exists, otherwise one without the other wouldn't mean much. Dualism thus reveals that each opposite serves a purpose and so is equally important.

It means that we should be grateful for our moments of darkness because without them we would fail to truly appreciate it when we finally stepped into the light. Experiencing scarcity enables us to appreciate abundance while helping us to avoid wastage. Only when we've suffered hunger are we able to value the food in our possession.

When we've experienced sadness we are able to appreciate joy, when we've experienced failure we are able to value success, we appreciate faithfulness after we've experienced betrayal, and we value people more after we've experienced the loss of loved ones. Bad experiences can be good in the long run when handled positively, because through such we are able to better appreciate the opposites of each bad experience. Bad experiences can also be good in another way. They could help us become more empathetic and sympathetic to other people when they go through similar experiences as we've been through. A person, for instance, who has experienced hunger would understand what hunger is and stands a better chance of being compassionate to someone experiencing hunger. Same goes for other experiences such as, bereavement, loss of employment, loss of property, broken relationships, failed marriages, poverty, sickness, and other misfortunes, we become more sympathetic and empathetic towards others with similar experiences after we've experienced them ourselves.

We should therefore be grateful for every circumstance and experience, good or bad, because each of them serves a beneficial purpose.

Musing

Imagine a life where only goodness existed. While it might seem blissful the truth is that it would both be boring and meaningless because nothing would make sense. If we had nothing to compare another thing with then we couldn't place the right value on the thing in question. The existence of an opposite or contrast makes the original thing meaningful and thus valuable too. There are lessons in every experience whether good or bad and it is possible that we experience bad things in life so that we can truly value the good things in life.

Could you be underappreciating your misfortunes?

70

Do It!

Now, the present, is what counts most because now is all we've got. Yesterday is gone and cannot be recalled while tomorrow is not certain and may never come. To get the best out of life we need to make the most of every moment and situation. When a moment passes it is lost for ever, leaving us only with memories but that is if we utilised such moment for anything worth remembering. We might be hurrying to get to work on a given morning and perhaps are running late, but that isn't a reason to fail to appreciate the freshness and beauty of the morning. We might be driving or commuting on a bus or train but it is up to us to take in the beauty of our surroundings no matter how chaotic. Many precious moments are wasted in life oftentimes through neglect due to one distracting preoccupation or another. We could build an enviable collection of precious memories from our daily morning commute to work if we are careful enough to let go and to enjoy the experience. Even the times we spend at home each day doing the regular things we do are loaded with opportunities for precious moments, but oftentimes we allow ourselves to get carried away by the seeming monotony of life that we fail to realise the uniqueness of each of those activities that we repeat on a daily basis. The beauty of life is fully appreciated when we take time to be in each moment as we encounter them, which wouldn't simply happen on its own except we decided to do so.

Similarly, we also need to make the most of now when it comes to pursuing our dreams and visions. There is always something that could be done now about our big ambitions, meaning that we don't have to wait for the elusive right time before acting on our desires or visions.

With writing, for instance, we could start now by putting down sketches of our thoughts and inspiration as they come instead of waiting till we feel ready before we did anything about our intention. Likewise, we don't have to wait till we are unemployed before we did anything about our desire to start a new business based on our passion. While holding down a job or more we could start researching the line of business of our interest to acquaint ourselves with the key things we need to know about the business. We could even start putting some money aside now for the capital requirement of the business instead of waiting for when we feel ready before we start looking around for the money needed.

Not having enough time, money, or qualification is not enough reason not to do something about our dreams and ambitions nor is it able to prevent us from acting on our intentions. We only need to be determined and driven enough to take the first steps no matter how little, and we will see that as we do what could be done now doors of new opportunities would be opened for us to keep us progressing till our dreams are realised. Rome as they say, was not built in a day but it started on a day and with a small step. Brick upon brick is how a skyscraper is built, as they say, little drops of water make a mighty ocean. We call all do something now about our big ideas, at least we could start by first laying down a plan and see where that takes us. Do it.

Musing

A wise man once said that the graveyard is the wealthiest place on earth, because in it are buried loads of unused skills, talents, potentials, and unrealised dreams, visions, and ambitions. If the graveyard is the richest place on earth, procrastination is largely responsible for its wealth. Dreams don't die naturally but instead people fail to realise them. Procrastination is a far bigger threat to dreams and ambitions than fear, lack of confidence, or lack of financial resources. Procrastination is a thief and a killer, it quietly steals our time while making us believe we still have more than enough time, until there's no longer any time left for it to steal. Procrastination tells us to sit by and do nothing till the perfect time comes, but there is no time named "perfect," instead we make each and any time perfect for what we have to do. As Nike's slogan goes, if there's something need doing, "Just Do It!" don't wait. Could you be waiting for the elusive perfect time?

71

One Day

One day begins and ends a story, a day is all it takes for history to be made whether good or bad. One day we are conceived in the womb and one day we emerge from the womb to start living. Finally, one day we die and retire from living into eternity. And, in between being born and dying, no matter what we experience or encounter, no matter how good or bad, and no matter how enduring or pleasuring, the power of one day is constantly demonstrated as we journey through life. Historically, one day was all it took to begin the end of such ignominies as transatlantic slavery, colonisation, and the Holocaust, which also all officially ended one day. One day, people who had been enslaved for centuries regained their freedom; one day, people who were hunted and killed by the Third Reich were free; and one day, the brutal apartheid regime in South African was brought to an end.

Biblically, one day was also what it took to turn the misfortunes of certain notable characters bringing them to a better place experientially. One day, Abraham who had been childless for many years had a son, subsequently having more sons, and many sons thus ending his childlessness. One day, Abraham's grandson Joseph who was wrongly imprisoned, having previously been enslaved, regained his freedom and everything he had lost to become a top officer in ancient Egypt. One day, Job who lost almost everything he had including his children and riches, was fully and better restored.

The power of one day represents the power of hope. It means that regardless of how bad or how long a situation may be one day is all it will take for things to turn around. As the saying goes, no condition is permanent. May we therefore be encouraged knowing that the things we encounter in life have come to pass but not to remain forever. It means then that we must never give up hope simply because we have encountered stormy waters, or wish death upon ourselves because life has dealt us constant deadly blows, because whatever it is will come to an end one day. We thus need to keep hope alive by encouraging ourselves and by doing whatever is necessary and possible including seeking divine help and guidance till that day arrives and change comes.

Musing

A tree does not make a forest as one season does not define a year, but history is made on a single day leaving the world transformed for a very long time. The power of one day cannot be overrated because it represents the power of hope. The saying, "where there is life there is hope" suggests that being alive holds out hope for recovery or improvement. Therefore, being alive is enough reason for us not to give up hope regardless of how things are. Ironically, where there is hope there is also life, because hope makes life bearable and worth living even when circumstances might make someone prefer death than life. We actually die when we stop hoping, although not literally, because, under certain circumstances, in the absence of hope life isn't worth living. Let the thought of one day keep your hope alive. Could you be ignoring the power of hope?

72

⚜

Broken

Life oftentimes leaves us broken due to one unpleasant experience
or another. Difficult relationships, where we seem to have tried our
best to make things work but our best falls short of expectation
resulting in no meaningful positive change, attritions arising from
the vicissitudes of life, despair and disappointment due to betrayal by
loved and trusted friends and family, and perplexity as a result of
being misunderstood or our good intentions being misconstrued could
leave us broken in life, and sometimes so broken that it is very difficult
picking up ourselves and holding things together. Likewise, parental
difficulties, business failures, long term unemployment, and serious
health challenges could also contribute to brokenness in life.
Brokenness is inevitable and isn't usually due to personal faults or
shortcomings, but could happen to anyone including the best and
strongest of us.

Although brokenness hurts, it could also be beneficial when
handled rightly and positively. Certain situations that leave us broken
also help to make us gentle and humble, especially circumstances that
strip us of those things we rely upon to feel important and better than

other people such as nice jobs and nice material possessions. When we are stripped of our lofty titles and possessions, and are reduced to simply being humans, we often become humble and humane.

Brokenness could also open us to being more compassionate towards other people especially those who might not be as privileged as we are or had been, thus making us able to sympathise and empathise as the case may be.

What then should we do when we find ourselves broken? Become mean, embittered, and hateful? Not at all. Become disconsolate, despaired, or depressed? No we shouldn't. Resign to fate and stay perpetually broken? Absolutely not. First, we must understand that no condition in life is permanent, therefore, brokenness is only for a while except we decide to prolong it through mismanagement. We should endeavour to allow the circumstances we pass through in life also pass through us. When we do, every circumstance would, by passing through us, transform and renew us into better persons by dealing with the part of our nature each circumstance was purposed to help us make better. For instance, arrogance could be transformed to humility, impatience to patience, intolerance to tolerance, apathy to empathy, hate to love, fear to trust, low self-esteem to confidence, and cowardice to courage. When we allow our circumstances to also pass through us as we pass through them, they will cleanse and purge us leaving us better than we were previously. Remember that in order to make something new from the old, the old is first broken before being remade into the new. Brokenness could and should result in new and better us.

Musing

In Japan, kintsukuroi is the process of repairing broken objects with gold. The flaw is seen as a unique piece of the object's history, which adds to its beauty. Brokenness makes us more beautiful than we were previously but only when we allow ourselves to be repaired with gold; when we allow ourselves become transformed as a result by replacing faulty nature or attitudes with admirable and precious virtues. Let the prospect of a more beautiful you inspire you through your brokenness, such that instead of becoming bitter you allow yourself to become better.

Could you be viewing your brokenness from a wrong perspective?

73

So, I Cry

Crying is often associated with weakness and thus isn't much encouraged in societies which emphasise masculinity. When, for instance, young boys cry publicly they are usually teased for being "sissies" because of conventional attitude towards crying. In some cultures, men are almost forbidden to cry, especially publicly, because it is believed to be a demonstration of weakness or cowardice. Crying, in some cultures, is also wrongly perceived as a demonstration of guilt, when an accused person breaks down as a result of physical and emotional torment and abuse. Consequently, people raised under such cultures are trained to stifle their emotions and to hold back their tears even in circumstances where it is human and natural to cry. Such denial of oneness the need to relieve an emotion through crying is unhealthy even in the short run. And is even more harmful to a person's health in the long run especially where people have mastered the act of suppressing their emotions and refusing to cry when circumstances call for it, due to upbringing.

Refusing to cry when we should, amongst other things, could result in increased heartbeat, heavy breathing, increased stress level, sadness, distress, despair, and depression in the long run, none of which is good for our health. On the other hand, suppression our emotions could leave us hardened, desensitised, insensitive, or apathetic, all of which are harmful to our emotional wellbeing. Interestingly, science shows that crying has its benefits both to the human body and mind.

Reflex tears clear debris, such as smoke and dust from the eyes; continuous tears lubricate the eyes helping protecting them from infection; while emotional tears, which contain stress hormones and other toxins, help detoxify the body by flushing these hormones and toxins out of our system. Crying also helps to self-soothe, dulls pain, improves mood, helps recover from grief, and helps restore emotional balance. These and more benefits are lost when we stifle our emotions and refuse to cry.

Personally, I was raised in one of those cultures where crying publicly for men was frowned at as a sign of weakness. So I grew up mastering my emotions especially publicly, but at a cost. Without realising it I was gradually losing the freedom of being able to express my emotions publicly where and when necessary, with the unpleasant result of having to bottle my emotions. So, while, for instance, I withheld my tears publicly it was inside and in private that I cried, but mostly inside. Fortunately, after a series of circumstances in middle adulthood left me broken, I found myself crying publicly unintentionally and unrestrained. Being broken had set me free! It was a liberating experience being able to let my tears flow freely, although somewhat embarrassing at times but nonetheless very rewarding. I felt human! I cried in empathy for others, I cried in sympathy for others, and I felt other's pains. I became truly human! Ironically, I became a man when I was finally able to cry, privately and publicly. I became a new man, a real man! I felt different, I felt alive, I felt free. I am still free!

Musing

*Did you know that only humans of all creatures cry? We are the only
species capable of expressing emotions through crying and shedding tears.
Perhaps there is very good reason for that. But even if not, wouldn't it be a
shame if we failed to avail ourselves of this ability which only humans
possess? It is as good, healthy, and wholesome to cry when occasion demands
so as it is bad, unhealthy, and unwholesome not to cry when we should. It is
also not a sign of weakness or cowardice to cry publicly as a man if in crying
we are being true to our inner feelings. This is why I now let my tears flow
freely when necessary, privately or publicly. I suggest you do too.*

Could you be damaging your health by trying to be masculine?

74

Wisdom

Who is a wise person? Wisdom is defined as the quality of having experience, knowledge, and good judgement. In recent times, more emphasis has been placed on the good judgement aspect of the definition of wisdom, leading to a refined definition of wisdom as not merely possessing knowledge but rightly applying knowledge. Wisdom is not just knowing what to say or do (knowledge) but knowing when and how to say or do that thing and actually saying or doing it at the right time, place, and how best to do it. The right application of knowledge, therefore, is wisdom. Which makes sense because to know and not do is truly not to know. The importance and purpose of knowledge is in the application.

Foolishness, the opposite of wisdom, is also defined as the lack of good sense or judgement. Since we all demonstrate some degree of lack of good sense or judgement, is it right then to say that we are all foolish? Likewise, since we also all demonstrate some degree of good sense or judgement, can we all be said to be wise?

This is where the concept of the wise-fool comes in.

Although, arguably, we all have the ability to show good and bad sense or judgement at different times, we do so in various degrees. With some people their sense of good judgement greatly outweighs their sense of bad judgement or they show more good judgement than bad judgement on a general basis. Are these the wise people? On the other hand, there are people whose sense of bad judgement outweighs their sense of good judgement or people who generally show more sense of bad judgement than good judgement. Are these the foolish people? It becomes obvious that wisdom and foolishness are not necessarily mutually exclusive because where one abides abundantly the other is likely to be found even if only in meagre quantity.

The famous Greek fabulist Aesop, whose collection of fables and stories are legendary, is synonymous with wisdom because of the wisdom in his tales. Aesop is generally regarded as a very wise man and while this is true going by the wisdom of his fables, his death was caused by his show of bad judgement or, in other word, by his foolishness. King Croesus, who was amazed by Aesop's smart wit, sent him to Delphi on a mission. Whereas Aesop's wisdom had been widely appreciated in every country he had been, the Delphinians didn't seem impressed by him. In response, Aesop insulted the Delphinians who subsequently kicked him out of their city but not before hiding a consecrated item from a temple in his belongings thus incriminating him. Aesop was eventually accosted as he made his way home, arrested, tried, and condemned to death for blasphemy and desecration. He was eventually thrown off a cliff to his death. Thus the wise Aesop met his death as a result of own foolishness. A wise-fool?

Musing

Wisdom is a necessity in life, through wisdom relationships are built and effectively managed. Relationships are a vital aspect of human life because almost everything we do is based on a type of relationship. Relationship underlies our daily living through our associations and interactions from the family, neighbourhood, community, country, to the world at large; from the academic institutions we attend to our places of work; and from the social associations to religious groups we belong to. Almost every problem we encounter in life can be effectively dealt with if we exercised discretion and good judgement. Families have been torn apart, lives wasted, properties destroyed, and wars fought between persons and nations all because of poor judgement. Thus, we have need to show good sense or judgement at least most of the time if we cannot all the time.

Could you need to exercise more good judgement in your relationships?

75

Ignorance

It is often said that ignorance is bliss but this is only one half of the quotation it comes from. The quotation in full is from Thomas Gray's poem "Ode on a Distant Prospect of Eton College" (1742) and goes: "Where ignorance is bliss, 'tis folly to be wise." It suggests that ignorance is only bliss on occasions where it is unnecessary or dangerous to be wise. Ignorance is defined as the lack of knowledge or information. Thus, ignorance cannot generally be bliss because not knowing what we should know cannot rightly be considered a delight.

It is good and necessary for us to know the things we should know, and it is unnecessary knowing what we don't need to know. Knowledge places a huge burden on us because when we know, we feel the need to act based on what we know but it isn't always everything we know that we are able to do something about. Hence the burden of knowledge.

In the underworld people are hunted and killed simply for being privy to a secret they weren't supposed to know. Ignorance would be bliss in such circumstances because it could've saved the lives of such people. I once asked a question on Facebook about what people would do if there was nothing they couldn't do. A young man responded that he would love to see what was in the minds of people, to which I replied that if he did he might wish he never did. Relationships would be more difficult and perhaps untenable if we all knew what was in the mind of everyone. Living might even become unbearable for all of us. There is much truth and wisdom in the idiom, "What you don't know can't hurt you." Although, in some cases, it is possible to get hurt because we didn't know what we ought to know.

Gossip is one way we often get to know those things we don't really need to know, and it is a great destroyer of relationships. Sadly, gossips are not always entirely truthful but are usually presented from the gossiper's perspective often with malicious intent. Therefore, gossips are not to be relied upon but, unfortunately, we often believe and act on them. It often is the case that people's attitude towards other people change based only what they've heard about those other people, even though what they heard could be entirely or partly wrong. Wisdom, therefore, is in discerning what we should and shouldn't know, and ensuring that we know what we should know while ignoring the things we don't need to know even when we come across such information through gossip or any other means.

Musing

Good relationships make for a better quality of life and living. Good relationships are founded on love, trust, and tolerance. Relationships don't come as good or bad but instead they are made either good or bad through how they are managed. Tolerance is an effective tool for the effective management of relationships. Good relationships aren't without issues, problems or misunderstandings but what makes them good is how these things are handled by the parties involved. Knowing when and what to let go and when and what to hold onto is very important. Discerning what and what not to know is also very important but, more important is ignoring what we don't need to know even when we happen to know.

Could you be holding on to something that isn't necessary for you to know?

76

Zombies

Arthur Fletcher, former head of the United Negro College Fund, coined the popular phrase, "A mind is a terrible thing to waste." Colloquially, a zombie refers to someone who is "braindead," although not literally. Zombies are people who fail to use their brains but instead simply conform to popular trends and fads. Hence this equally popular quotation which is credited to an unknown source, "Zombies eat brains, you are safe." The message here is that if you haven't got any brains (or don't make use of your brains) then you need not fear zombies (who in this case refers to imaginary revived corpses commonly known as the "living-dead"). Being referred to as a zombie isn't a compliment at all but instead is a form of derogation. No one would like to be called a zombie but no one should also behave as one.

Going by what obtains in our world today, particularly in cyberspace, it would seem that some people (perhaps a majority) are gradually being turned into zombies. A significant number of social media users simply forward or share messages or posts they've received or seen either because they were requested to do so or they believe the information therein to be accurate. Nowadays not many people care to independently verify the authenticity and accuracy of the myriad of information circulating online before either accepting them as credible and true or going on to take corresponding actions. Consequently, some people have accepted as fact false information put out by suspicious sources (including instituted authorities) and for the purpose of misinforming the public perhaps in pursuance of a hidden diabolical agenda. Thus the internet, especially social media, seems to have succeeded the traditional media as a formidable brainwashing and misinformation tool. The success of this weapon is revealed in the extent to which the public trust and rely on social media as their source for news and other information. Hence the high degree of misinformation prevalent in the global village which is home to all of us.

Also, the amount of time people spend on social media on a daily basis is so unhealthy that it has become something of a distraction.

Such excessive indulgence in social media makes zombies of its victims, who instead of living life in the real world exist in a virtual world far removed from reality. The dire consequence is that the real world, having been deserted, is deprived of mindful people, leaving zombies to roam free.

Musing

Our mind is one of our most prized possessions because it enables us to think, and the ability to think accords us individuality and independence. Possessing a mind, however, isn't enough because if we failed to rightly use our minds then we are no different to creatures without minds; the same way refusing to use our brains is tantamount to being brainless, braindead, or zombies. Using our minds rightly would require us to think for ourselves independently and originally, free from any form of conditioning or control, such that our thoughts and consequent actions are independently and originally ours and not products of manipulation and undue external influences. Using our minds rightly would also require us to carefully verify the accuracy and authenticity of every information, regardless of its source, before accepting it and acting on it. It would also require us to do only the things we know are right for us to do and not to do things simply because we are instructed or required to do so. If we desire to live the lives that we are meant to live, we need to rightly use our minds. We need to ensure that we don't become zombies.

Could you be behaving like a zombie in some ways?

77

Wake Up!

"Woke" is a term commonly used in today's world, in reference to people who have become aware of some uncommon knowledge related to one or another aspect of life in the world, particularly social injustice and inequality. The degree of misinformation, manipulation, and deception prevalent in the world is so much that it is like a strong sedative used to induce humanity to sleep. Hence the need for us to rouse ourselves from sleep and awake from slumber. The educational system only partially informs, thus relying on it for education is a big risk. The origin and history of humanity, for instance, is relegated to specialised disciplines offered only at higher institutions. Consequently, the African origin of humans is uncommon knowledge. Similarly, a significant aspect of African and world history has remained hidden while distorted versions of history have been made popular, mainly through the educational system, in pursuance of different agendas. Ancient and modern history of the world is presented from the single perspective of Western sources as though accurate even though every story has different perspectives and can only be complete when every perspective has been taken into account.

History is not the only aspect of our lives that has been subjected to distortion and misinformation, but it stands out because of its significance and relevance. The importance of history is underscored by these quotations: "Those who don't know history are destined to repeat it." (Edmund Burke); "A people without the knowledge of their past history, origin and culture is like a tree without roots." (Marcus Garvey); and, "If you don't know history, then you don't know anything. You are a leaf that doesn't know it is part of a tree." (Michael Crichton). Our poor knowledge of the past is largely responsible for the present state of the world. Another reason is the complacency which has made us too trusting and overly dependent on official sources (e.g., governmental, organisational) for our information and education. Sadly, the diabolical agendas responsible for misinformation in the world are championed by governments and other instituted authorities.

On a good note, the internet has now made it possible and easier to unearth previously hidden information and resources including historical records and research findings based on objective studies. The onus is thus on us to avail ourselves of this refreshing development and properly and rightly educate ourselves in addition to whatever formal education (or miseducation) we have received. Note, however, that our proper education would require a significant degree of unlearning some if the wrong things we have learned and believed to be true. The deception has gone on for so long causing us to be asleep for too long. The clarion call is for us to wake up!

Musing

Imagine a world where everyone is a guinea pig in a social experiment but all are completely unaware that this is the case. So, the people engage in normal living activities not knowing that their actions are not entirely their own but instead the result of programming and conditioning. Imagine that this imaginary world is the real world we live in and you wouldn't be too far from the truth. The good news is that this status quo could change but for that to happen we need to take personal responsibility to break free from the experimental process and live as we truly ought to. We need to wake up! Could you be sleep-walking through life?

Other Books By Ziri Dafranchi

**OTHER BOOKS
BY
ZIRI DAFRANCHI**

WILDERNESS FRUITS
ECLECTIC POEMS AND MUSINGS
(VOLUME 1)

The first book of the WILDERNESS FRUITS series; a novel combination of eclectic poems, traditional fables and short stories, and musings by the author with practical, applicable and inspirational encouragement. The fruits from a personal wilderness experience.

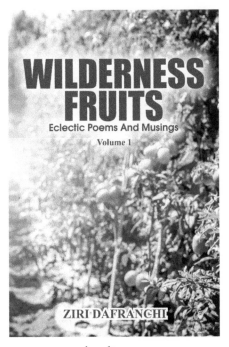

www.hereditaspress.com

MANNA
FOOD FOR THE SOUL
(VOLUME 1)
The first book of the MANNA series; the first in the devotional
genre to combine poetic meditations and regular devotionals into
digestible topics of faith, making it easier for you to choose and feast
on what your soul craves.

www.hereditaspress.com

MANNA
FOOD FOR THE SOUL
(VOLUME 2)

The second installment of the MANNA series; the first in the devotional genre to combine poetic meditations and regular devotionals into digestible topics of faith, making it easier for you to choose and feast on what your soul craves.

www.hereditaspress.com

LIFE
A MYSTERY SOLVED
(Revised And Updated)

The captivating philosophical nonfiction with answers to many of life's most controversial questions. Book One of the Trilogy of Truth.

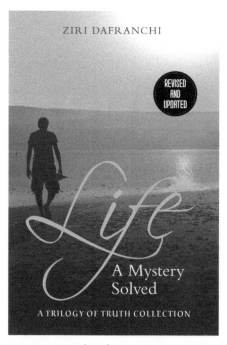

www.hereditaspress.com

BEING BLACK
REDISCOVERING A LOST IDENTITY

The deeply revealing truth about the hidden identity of some of today's Black people. Book Two of the Trilogy of Truth.

www.hereditaspress.com

PAGAN WORLD
DECEPTION AND FALSEHOOD IN RELIGION

The bold revelation about religion based on the present concept as a human rather than divine invention. Book Three of the Trilogy of Truth.

www.hereditaspress.com

Milton Keynes UK
Ingram Content Group UK Ltd.
UKHW010640040324
438885UK00001B/174